Grandpa
and the horse

by Ben Butterworth
pictures by Lorraine Calaora

Nelson

'I am tired,' Father said.

'And I am tired,' Mother said.

'I am very tired,' Trog said.

'I am the most tired,' said Grandpa.
'I would love a ride.'

'So would I,' Mother said.

'And I would,' Father said.

'And I would,' Trog said.
'I would love a ride
on Grandpa's back.'

4

'Oh, no you don't!'
said Grandpa Gripe.
'Nobody is going to ride on me.'

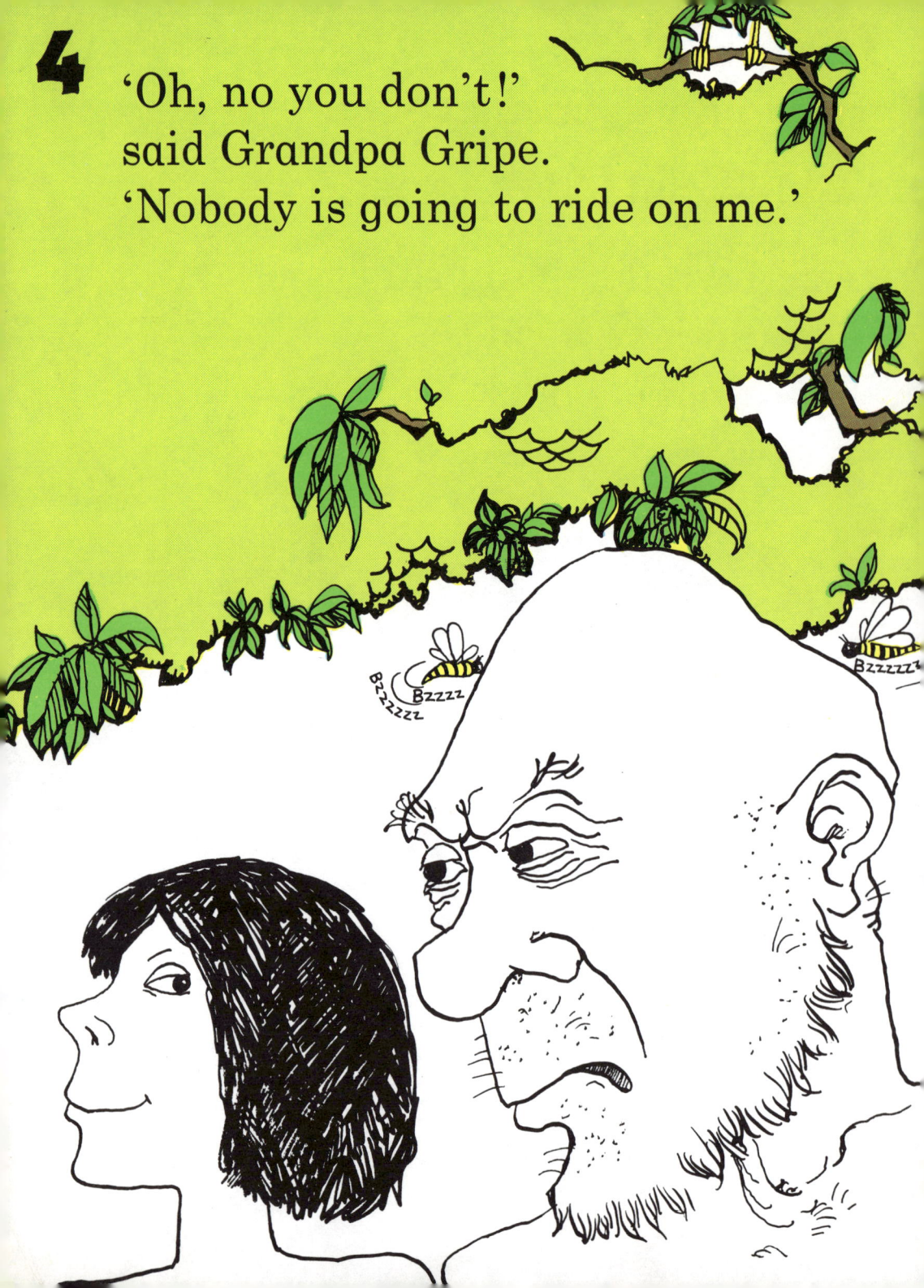

Bzzzzzz Bzzzz

Bzzzzzz

'The Quickerwits are never tired,'
Mother said to Grandpa.
'They ride.
They ride on horses.
They catch a wild horse
and ride on its back!'

'If the Quickerwits
can catch a wild horse, so can I,'
said Grandpa Gripe.
'Then I can ride on its back.'

'Yes, you catch one,' said Father.

'Yes, catch one,' Trog said,
'and I can ride it too!'

Grandpa went to the hills
to catch his horse.
He saw a good one
and ran to catch it.

He ran fast, but the horse ran too.

Grandpa ran faster,

but the horse ran faster as well.

Grandpa went back home.

'Trog,' he said,
'go and ask the Quickerwits
how they catch wild horses.
Wild horses can run faster
than I can.
I'm worn out.'

Trog went
to the land of the Quickerwits.

'How do you catch a wild horse?'
he asked.

'It's easy,' they said.
'It's very easy.
We make a lasso.
We throw it over the horse's head
and hold on to the rope.
Then the horse cannot get away.'

Trog went home.
He and Father made a lasso
for Grandpa.

Grandpa went back to the hills
to catch his horse.
He saw one and ran after it.
He threw the lasso.

The lasso went over the horse's head,
but Grandpa's end of the rope
was caught round his leg.
He was pulled flat on his back.

The wild horse pulled Grandpa
up the hills and down,
down the hills and up,
into the river
and out the other side.

'Stop him!' shouted Grandpa.

'Stop him!'

Help meeeeeeee......

Father and Trog ran to help.
They set Grandpa free
and the horse ran away.

'Well,
you caught a horse,' Father said.

'Yes, you did,' Trog said.

'I did not catch a horse,'
said Grandpa Gripe.
'The horse caught me.'